Causes of the American Revolution

by Randi Reisfeld
and Jackie Robb

Table of Contents

4   Introduction
Down with Tyranny!

6   Chapter 1
Social and Political Causes of the Revolution
Who were the colonists, and what social and political factors paved their road to independence?

18   Chapter 2
Economic Causes of the Revolution
What economic factors led the colonies to seek self-rule?

30   Cartoonist's Notebook:
Loyalty or Rebellion?

32   Chapter 3
Ideological Causes of the War
What were the new ideas influencing people's thoughts about their right to independence?

Conclusion: A Triumphant Choice . . . page 42

How to Write an Argument . . . . page 44

Glossary . . . . page 46

Index . . . . page 48

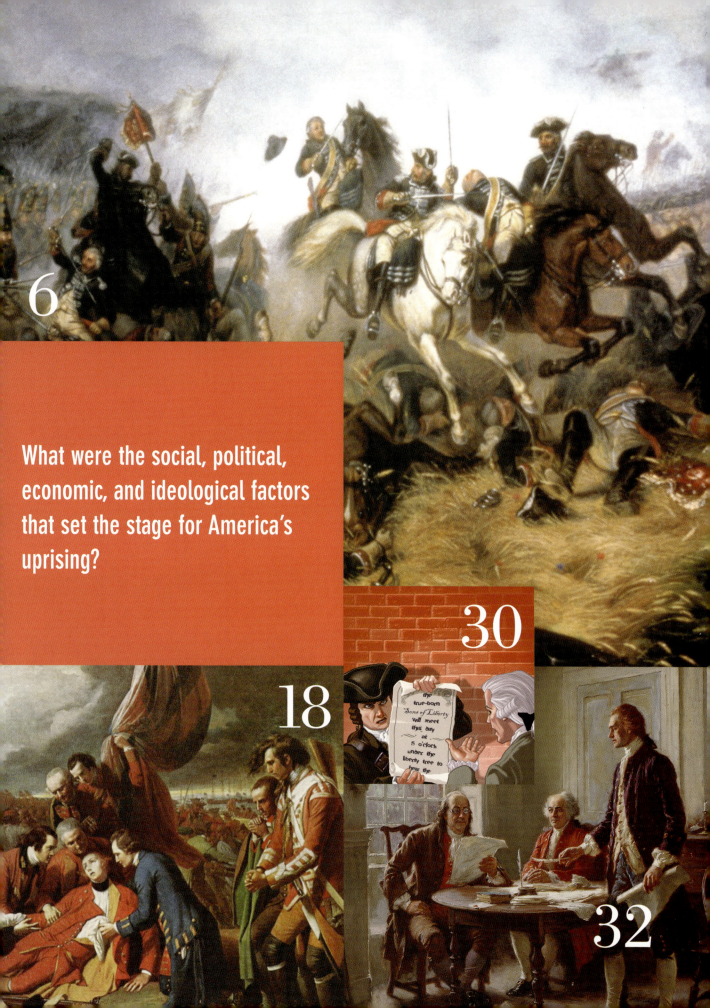

6

What were the social, political, economic, and ideological factors that set the stage for America's uprising?

18

30

32

The first shots of the American Revolution were fired on April 19, 1775, at the Battles of Lexington and Concord when British troops were sent to destroy arms that were being stored by the colonial militia on a farm outside Boston.

Introduction

Down with Tyranny!

Early on the morning of April 19, 1775, the British king, George III, was at home in London. At the same time, across the Atlantic Ocean, the first shot was fired at the Battle of Lexington, Massachusetts. When the news arrived, King George was outraged. Now Great Britain faced results in the American colonies of actions taken and decisions made earlier by the king.

▲ **King George III in 1775**

King George III had ruled Great Britain since 1760. The king controlled every colony ruled by England around the globe, including the American colonies. King George III had come to power during the French and Indian War, which the British won in 1763. Because fighting the war was not cheap, England now had a debt.

The king needed to pay back the money that England owed. Laws already existed that allowed King George to charge the colonies special taxes, called duties, or tariffs. So King George began to tax the colonies. Many colonists refused to pay the taxes. The king thought the money raised by the taxes would help the colonists. The king wondered why the colonists would want to rebel.

PRIMARY SOURCE

Declaration of Rights and Grievances, 1774

After King George imposed the Intolerable Acts, the First Continental Congress met in Philadelphia and sent a Declaration of Rights and Grievances in 1774 in hopes of a peaceful resolution. You can read the original document online at the Library of Congress website, www.loc.gov.

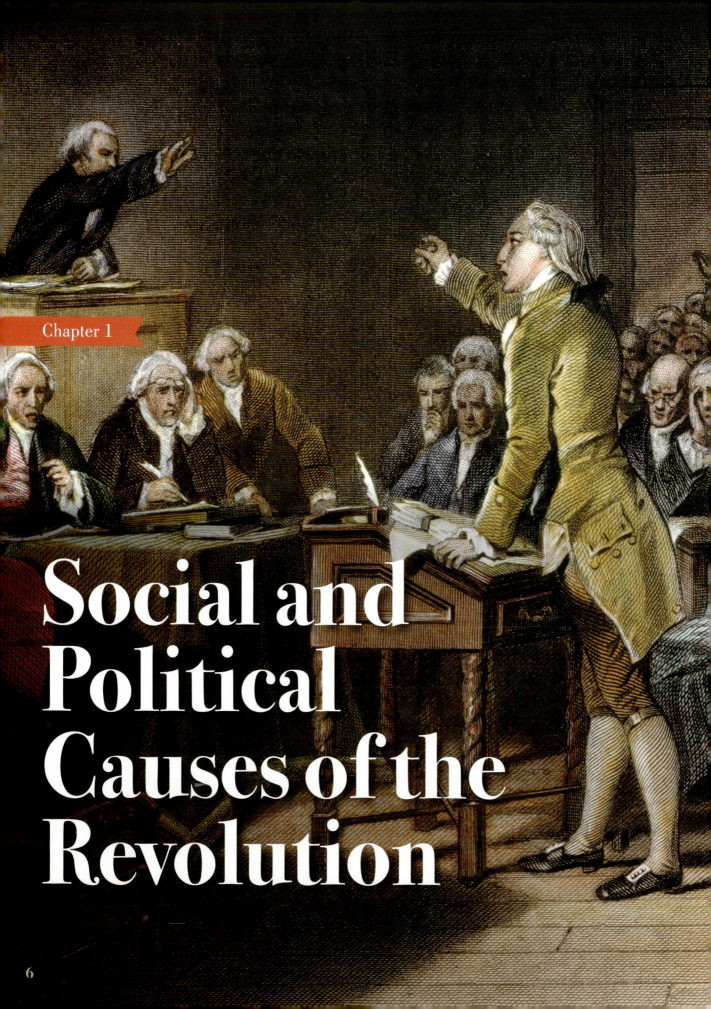

Chapter 1

Social and Political Causes of the Revolution

Who were the colonists, and what social and political factors paved their road to independence?

ESSENTIAL VOCABULARY

- banishment — page 10
- frontier — page 12
- indentured servant — page 11
- Loyalist — page 14
- monarchy — page 8
- Patriot — page 14
- persecution — page 8
- Pilgrim — page 8
- prosperity — page 11
- revolution — page 16
- theocracy — page 10
- theologian — page 10
- tolerance — page 10

▲ New Hampshire, Massachusetts, Rhode Island, Connecticut, New York, New Jersey, Pennsylvania, Delaware, Maryland, Virginia, North Carolina, South Carolina, and Georgia made up the thirteen original colonies.

The people who rose up against the British crown in 1775 were a mixed group. Some of the people descended from European settlers who came to North America in the 1600s. Other people, who arrived later, were born in Europe. Over the years, England issued several charters to the colonies. A charter gave companies and other groups the right to settle lands in North America. In 1606, the Virginia colony received the first charter. Early settlements also created colonial governments.

Chapter 1

Governing the Colonies

Great Britain was what is called a constitutional **monarchy** (MAH-nar-kee). In a monarchy form of government, a king or queen rules with the help of an assembly of representatives. In Great Britain this group was called the Parliament (PAR-lih-ment). Together, King George and Parliament governed the American colonies. But the colonies were far from England, so the colonists largely governed the colonies.

The House of Burgesses

In the 1600s and 1700s colonists could find more economic success and self-government in some colonies than in others. The colonies with more success attracted the most settlers. For example, Jamestown in Virginia failed until the colony made serious changes. In 1619 the settlement established a House of Burgesses (BER-jeh-sez). The House of Burgesses was the first representative assembly in the colonies. The colonists who could vote elected the representatives. The governor of the colony kept great control. But the House of Burgesses gave the Virginia colonists a role in the government. At the time, the French, Spanish, and Dutch colonies did not make the same types of decisions about government.

The Mayflower Compact

In 1620 a ship called the *Mayflower* sailed from England for "northern Virginia." The passengers hoped to

land at the mouth of the Hudson River. Instead, the ship landed where Plymouth, Massachusetts, is today. In England, people followed the teachings of the Church of England. Many of the *Mayflower* passengers had different religious beliefs and were treated badly in England. Bad treatment, called **persecution** (per-sih-KYOO-shun), caused people to flee. Today the *Mayflower* passengers are known as the **Pilgrims** (PIL-grimz). The Pilgrims were also called Separatists (SEH-puh-rih-tists).

The Pilgrims dreamed of finding a new home where people could worship freely. Plymouth had no charter. So the Pilgrims wrote a set of rules for the settlement at Plymouth. The rules make up the Mayflower Compact. The rules in the compact are the first written framework of government in the British colonies. The compact outlined the commitment to governing of the colonies by the colonists.

Social and Political Causes of the Revolution

▲ The intended course of the *Mayflower* would have taken the ship to what is now New York Harbor, but, off by just a few degrees, the ship landed in what is now Cape Cod, Massachusetts.

PRIMARY SOURCE

The original Mayflower Compact is believed to be lost. However, a copy of it appears in Plymouth governor William Bradford's handwritten history *Of Plymouth Plantation*, around 1630.

THEN AND NOW

The Town Meeting

The first town meeting was held by the Puritans in Massachusetts in 1633. Town meetings are still considered one of the purest forms of democracy. When a decision had to be made in the village, the leaders would call a town meeting. Though at first only men could attend and only freemen could vote, over time this forum became a place where every member of the community could voice his or her opinion. Through these meetings, the Puritans helped establish democratic ideals within their colonial culture.

▲ A town meeting is a democratic forum that originated in New England. To this day, town meetings are still held in many states.

Chapter 1

Growth and Expansion

New Seekers of Tolerance

After the Pilgrims, the Puritans (PYER-ih-tunz) also fled religious persecution. Both groups were in search of religious tolerance (TAH-luh-runs), or acceptance. But both groups did not always treat others with tolerance. In fact, the Pilgrims and Puritans established strict **theocracies** (thee-AH-kruh-seez) in the colonies. In a theocracy, the church governs the people. In many cases the theocracies were very intolerant of new ideas and different beliefs. People who did not follow the teachings of the theocracy risked **banishment** (BA-nish-ment), or removal.

Many people banished to the wilderness died. Some of the banished colonists had enough determination (and resources and supporters) to start new colonies. One such colonist was Roger Williams, who founded a new settlement called Providence Plantation.

Roger Williams was a **theologian** (thee-uh-LOH-jun), or religious scholar, who believed in tolerance. The colony founded by Williams was a safe place for religious minorities. Williams believed in treating Native Americans with fairness and respect, and in abolishing slavery. Anne Hutchinson was another great theologian and leader. Massachusetts Bay Colony banished Hutchinson, who then settled Portsmouth, Rhode Island.

{ **The Root of the Meaning:** *theocracy* } comes from the Greek word *theokratia*, which means "rule of god."

In 1681, William Penn founded Pennsylvania. Penn wanted to form the first truly free and peaceful society. Penn wrote a document called the First Frame of Government that outlined the rights of Pennsylvania colonists. The document gave colonists freedom of enterprise so that people could start businesses. It provided for freedom of the press and religious tolerance. Colonists in Pennsylvania had the right to private property, and to a trial by jury. The First Frame of Government set up a two-house legislature to create and pass laws. As owner of Pennsylvania, Penn could veto laws passed by the legislature.

New Seekers of Opportunity

Many settlers came to America for religious freedom. For other settlers, the vast land and resources of America offered a chance to make money. The Dutch East India Company was the first company to trade goods throughout Europe and Asia. In 1609 the company hired the explorer Henry Hudson to find a northwest passage from Holland to India. For Henry Hudson, the passage through the Arctic was blocked by ice and the mission failed. However, Hudson did claim land for the Dutch and named the land New Netherland. Dutch settlers moved in quickly. New Netherland had plentiful wildlife, such as beavers and mink. In Europe there was a great demand for the fur of these animals, so suppliers in America made a lot of money. New Amsterdam, known now as Manhattan, became an important port for trading fur.

Dutch power in North America did not last long. The British saw the profit made by the Dutch settlement, so Britain decided to take over. In 1664 the British navy overpowered the Dutch in New Netherland. Quickly, the British renamed the colony New York. The name honored the brother of the king—James, Duke of York. (The Duke of York had planned the takeover.) The Dutch settlers stayed as new British settlers came to New York. All of the settlers lived together in peace and **prosperity** (prah-SPAIR-ih-tee), or wealth.

Some people could pay for the trip to the colonies. A person with less money might come to America as an indentured servant (in-DEN-cherd SER-vunt). Wealthy patrons, or masters, paid the fare and the cost of room and board. The indentured servant had to work for the patron for the length of the indenture. (The indenture was an agreed-upon amount of time, usually five to seven years.) At the end of the contract, the servant no longer had to work for the patron.

Checkpoint
Read More About It
Go to your local library or online to learn about the Dutch, French, and Spanish colonies in North America.

▼ The Dutch were skilled mapmakers. Their detailed sketches are still used by archaeologists today.

Chapter 1

The Moving Frontier

Over time, more and more Europeans settled the Americas. New settlers pushed out many Native American peoples who had been on the land for centuries. Some tribal groups and settlers made peace. But Native Americans and settlers regularly argued and fought over territory and resources. While some Native American tribes and settlers learned to cooperate, other tribes and settlers continued to mistreat one another.

Most Europeans settled near the coast of the Atlantic Ocean. The British built cities close to the rivers of New England and the Middle Atlantic colonies. Settlers founded villages on the rich farmland of the southern colonies. As the coastal areas grew more crowded, people moved further inland, pushing west to the edge of settlements, or the **frontier** (frun-TEER). Trading posts opened and small towns sprang up around the posts.

Settling the frontier was risky. Clearing the land to build was backbreaking work. Success or peace could not be promised. Battles between the Native Americans and the settlers over the use of land were brutal and bloody.

The French and Indian War (1754–1763)

In 1700 the population of the American colonies was about 250,000. By 1750 nearly 1.5 million people crowded the British colonies. So British colonists began moving into the Spanish and French colonies in North America. Soon, conflict began. The conflict became the French and Indian War. The British fought the French for control in North America. The British also fought Native American tribes who sided with the French. During the war, the colonial militias (mih-LIH-shuz), or local armies, worked together with the British. The French and Indian War was an important training ground for colonists. Ten years later, many of the militiamen would take up arms against the British king. The bloody conflict ended in 1763 with a British victory. In the peace treaty, North American land holdings by Britain doubled. However, the cost of victory was high. England felt the colonies ought to make sacrifices for the good of Britain, the "mother country."

Social and Political Causes of the Revolution

◀ The bows and arrows of Native Americans were often no match for the rifles and guns of the pioneers.

THEY MADE A DIFFERENCE

George Washington (1732–1799)

George Washington began his military career in the Virginia militia and is believed to have fired one of the first shots of the French and Indian War. His experience and training during that war helped shape the man into the military strategist he would become, giving him the skills to lead, fight, and win the American Revolution (1775–1783).

▲ France and Britain published different maps of their holdings and land claims in North America.

13

Chapter 1

Colonial Defiance

After the French and Indian War, the king and Parliament passed many laws that most colonists disliked. The laws included the Sugar Act of 1764 and the Quartering Act and Stamp Act of 1765. The Sugar Act taxed the sugar that colonists bought. The Quartering Act allowed British soldiers to live in the homes of colonists. The Stamp Act placed a tax on all printed papers. The cost of the taxes was small, but not having a say about taxes seemed unfair to the colonists.

Colonists called **Loyalists** (LOY-uh-lists) remained true to the British king and the Parliament. Loyalists accepted the new laws and taxes. Loyalists wanted to remain subjects of King George.

Many other colonists, however, disagreed with the new acts. The colonies had already done a lot for Great Britain. Colonists had governed the colonies for a long time. Colonial militias had helped fight and win the French and Indian War. Many colonists did not think Britain had the right to pass laws and orders without the consent of the colonies. Many disagreed with having a large military force from Britain in the colonies during peacetime.

Colonists who opposed the crown became known as **Patriots** (PAY-tree-uts). Patriots began speaking out against British actions. Patriots wrote pamphlets. They organized people to not buy certain goods, an action called a boycott (BOY-kaht), and also stopped trade. The British said the Patriots were involved in acts of treason. But the Patriots wanted change and continued to speak out and rebel.

A group of Boston shopkeepers and artisans organized a rebel group called the Sons of Liberty. The group protested British actions such as the Stamp Act.

Anti–Stamp Act cartoons and rhetoric warning against use of the stamps were printed in newspapers and handbills. ▶

Social and Political Causes of the Revolution

Soon every colony had a Sons of Liberty chapter. The Sons of Liberty wanted people involved with the Stamp Tax forced out of office. Although the group sometimes used violence, words were their best weapon. The group distributed their writing among the people. The Sons of Liberty wanted to educate colonists about the Patriot cause.

Discontent with the Stamp Act of 1765, which was to be used to pay for 10,000 troops along the Appalachian Frontier, led to its repeal in 1766. ▼

HISTORICAL PERSPECTIVE

Mercy Otis Warren (1728–1814)

Today women have positions of power in the political arena, but in the 1770s, it was rare to find a female among the cigar-smoking, tough-talking Founders. Enter Mercy Otis. She had no formal education but had been raised in a family that believed in freedom and was willing to fight for it.

Otis married James Warren, a well-known politician. It soon became clear that she was a better speechwriter than he was. She began writing books, speeches, and articles. Many of them were published anonymously, since she was a woman and writing what would be considered traitorous words against England. A strong believer in democracy, she wrote, "The happiness of mankind depends much on the modes of government."

▲ **This teapot, ironically made in England, is a celebration of the repeal of the Stamp Act.**

Chapter 1

In 1770, British troops in Boston killed several unarmed colonists after the colonists had thrown snowballs at the soldiers. Patriots called the tragedy the Boston Massacre (MA-sih-ker). In 1774, Britain closed the port of Boston. Parliament rewrote the Massachusetts charter and installed a military government. Colonists named the actions the Intolerable Acts. Unrest in the colonies reached a boiling point.

On September 5, 1774, representatives from every colony met in Philadelphia, Pennsylvania, at the First Continental Congress. The representatives wrote to the king and asked for a compromise, or agreement, that would bring peace. The king said

{ The Root of the Meaning: **revolution** }

comes from the Latin word *revolvere*, meaning "to turn." A revolution is a complete turn toward a new kind of future, and a turn away from the past.

that the colonies must either "submit or triumph." By the spring of 1775, fighting broke out between British soldiers and colonists. In July of 1776, the Continental Congress issued the Declaration of Independence. For the colonists, **revolution** (reh-vuh-LOO-shun), or revolt, became an option.

Summing Up

- The British colonies were settled by colonists in search of religious freedom, tolerance, and new opportunities for wealth and prosperity.

- They settled along the Eastern Seaboard and established separate governments under British rule, but they largely governed themselves from day to day.

- The colonies encountered hardships and competed for land and other resources with one another and the Native Americans who already lived there.

- After the French and Indian War, England finally began enforcing trade laws in the colonies, and resentment toward British tyranny eventually became a cry for battle.

Putting It All Together

Choose one of the following research activities. Work independently, in pairs, or in small groups. Share what you've learned with your class, and listen as others present their findings.

1. Draw a map of the American colonies in 1775. Label each colony. Research the origins of the people who settled each of the colonies and the type of colonial government they established, and define the characteristics of these governments.

2. Imagine you were a delegate at the First Continental Congress. Write an argument for the cause you are representing.

3. Visit your local library or go online to find information about the people who helped build your city and state. What Native American tribes first inhabited your region? Who were the settlers who later established communities in your area? What immigrant groups brought their customs and cultures to the place you call home? Write an essay or lecture or create a graphic poster that explains the lasting influences of these different groups.

Chapter 2

Economic Causes of the Revolution

The ports of New England kept trading ships busy, and the mills cranked out textiles.

What economic factors led the colonies to seek self-rule?

ESSENTIAL VOCABULARY

- broker   page 26
- imperial   page 26
- indigo   page 21
- mercantilism page 19
- oppression   page 24
- plantation   page 22
- tariff   page 19

Each colony grew or manufactured certain goods. Southern colonies grew rice, tobacco, and, eventually, cotton. Northern colonies had fisheries, fur-trading posts, and forests. Great Britain depended on colonial resources. The British also counted on the money earned from certain cash crops—crops grown for sale—in the colonies.

Mercantilism

England controlled colonial economies through a system called **mercantilism** (MER-kun-ty-lih-zum). In mercantilism, the colonies existed for the benefit of the colonial power. The colonial power tightly controlled all trade. So the American colonies were allowed to do business with England. But the colonists could trade with other countries only if England gave the colonies permission. When England did allow trade with other countries, the colonists were forced to pay large taxes on the traded goods, called **tariffs** (TAIR-ifs).

The colonists paid, but not happily. People wrote letters to newspapers and protested the unfair regulations. Steep taxes put restrictions on the money colonists could earn.

Chapter 2

The Middle Passage

Africa to America to Europe

In colonial times, slave traders captured people in Africa. The captured slaves were a valuable commodity, or good, worth a lot of money. The demand for slaves was high because slaves could provide labor, or work, for free. Traders moved slaves between continents through a system called the Triangle Trade.

Ships filled with manufactured goods left Europe, bound for Africa. In Africa merchants exchanged the goods for African slaves. Traders chained hundreds of slaves inside of the ship. The slaves had little food and water, and no light. In North America the traders sold slaves for high profits or exchanged slaves for raw materials. In England the raw materials could be turned into manufactured goods. Then the pattern began again. The whole system was called the "Middle Passage," meaning the voyage between continents.

PRIMARY SOURCE

Autobiography of a Slave

A slave named Olaudah Equiano related his experience of the Middle Passage in his autobiography *The Interesting Narrative of the Life of Olaudah Equiano*. He described the ship:

"The closeness of the place, and the heat of the climate, added to the number in the ship, which was so crowded that each had scarcely room to turn himself, almost suffocated us."

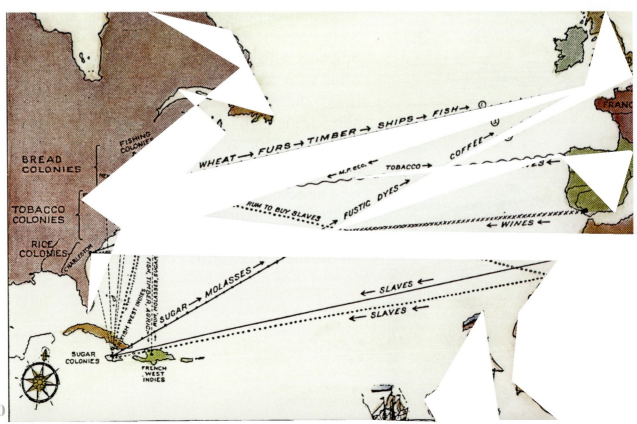

Economic Causes of the Revolution

The New England Economy

New England had a busy economy during the colonial period. The region was a major source of timber, or wood used for building. New Englanders used timber for building homes as well as ships and boats. The region also served as an important trading post.

In the time just before the American Revolution, the First Industrial Revolution took place in Europe. Soon after, people built factories in New England cities. Manufacturers brought wool from the South up to the North. In northern mills workers wove the wool into cloth.

Britain continued to control trade tightly. So New Englanders looked for new markets to sell manufactured goods. New Englanders also wanted markets for food products. The New England colonists began trading with the West Indies, another English colony. The West Indies sold molasses, sugar, and **indigo** (IN-dih-goh), a blue dye used to color clothing, to New England. England taxed the New England colonies for trading with places other than England. England added to the unfairness created by mercantilism in other ways. For example, England insisted that the colonists buy more from England than England bought from the colonies. The result was what is called an unequal balance of trade.

Life in the Mid-Atlantic

Farmers grew a wide range of foods in the rich soil of Pennsylvania, New Jersey, upstate New York, Delaware, and Maryland. Mid-Atlantic colonists exported food to Europe and the West Indies.

The Mid-Atlantic colonies had thickly wooded forests, as New England did. The forests provided wood for fuel, paper, and building supplies. Sawmills were a key business. Printing, publishing, and papermaking were important businesses. Shipbuilding companies also were important in the Mid-Atlantic colonies.

Industry in the region grew at a steady rate. Natural resources allowed the Mid-Atlantic colonies to produce a variety of goods to be sold. Broad rivers made it possible to transport goods to markets. Port cities, such as New York and Philadelphia, were centers of government, trade, and business.

◀ **The three points of the triangle were England, Africa, and the North American colonies.**

Chapter 2

HISTORICAL PERSPECTIVE

Plantations and Enslaved People

Life in the southern colonies was shaped by the Plantation Economy. A plantation is a large estate in which crops such as cotton, coffee, sugar, rice, and tobacco are grown. Sometime during the 1800s, the word *plantation* came to refer to the homes where wealthy landowners lived in grand style. That has long been the stereotype. However, a closer look at history proves that is not necessarily the case. There were many plantation-style farms in the South, but there were few wealthy plantation owners. Most were simple farmers. Still, even they relied on slaves to harvest their crops.

The South

In the southern colonies—Virginia, Georgia, and North and South Carolina—life seemed to move slowly. The land was lush and green. Temperatures were high in summertime. Farmers in New England struggled to plow the rocky soil. Southern farmers planted crops in rich, red clay that held moisture from the humid air. In the South the economy was built on rice and tobacco. Later, cotton became an important crop.

A family could not earn enough money by growing crops on a small piece of land. So some southern farmers built large farms called **plantations** (plan-TAY-shunz). Enslaved (in-SLAVED) Africans supplied the many hands needed to grow the rice and pick the tobacco leaves. Because the enslaved laborers were not paid, all profits went to the plantation owner. Enslaved labor became crucial to the survival of the South.

◀ The southern colonies relied on enslaved labor to help harvest massive amounts of rice, tobacco, and later cotton.

Economic Causes of the Revolution

▲ Many Native American tribes wanted the English to win the Revolutionary War in the hopes that white settlers would stop plundering their lands.

HISTORICAL PERSPECTIVE

The Iroquois Nation

Five Native American tribes—the Mohawk, Oneida, Onondaga, Cayuga, and Seneca—joined together to form an alliance. Calling themselves the Iroquois Nation, they had several goals.

Most important, they fought to protect themselves and the lands they inhabited, which stretched from New York State all the way up to Ontario, Canada.

They also hoped to succeed in commerce, the buying and selling of goods and services, with the newly arrived settlers from Europe.

Unlike most Native American tribes, they sided with Britain in what is called the French and Indian War, in which France and England fought over American colonial territory from 1754 to 1763. While most Native American tribes, having been treated unfairly by the British, sided with the French, the Iroquois Nation made a different decision. They believed that if Great Britain were to win the war, it would honor its friendship with the Iroquois and guarantee them land grants—something France was not prepared to do.

Then the American Revolution broke out. Most of the tribes remained loyal to Britain, but the Oneida broke away to side with the colonists. When the Americans won the war, General George Washington ordered that the tribes on the side of the English be destroyed. The few surviving Iroquois moved farther up into Canada. Later wars eventually led to the removal and transfer of all Native Americans to reservations.

23

Chapter 2

Intolerable Acts

In 1774 England passed a series of taxes called the Navigation Acts. Colonists changed the name to the Intolerable Acts. The colonists said the acts were a symbol of tyranny and unfair control, known as **oppression** (uh-PREH-shun). The new taxes were a burden for people throughout the colonies.

The tax money collected helped to pay for the huge British Empire, which included England. Most colonists thought of themselves as loyal British subjects. So taxes were accepted.

By the 1770s, however, taxes really began to hurt business in the colonies. Colonists believed the colonies should have proper representation in Parliament, which made the laws for all of Great Britain. The British believed the colonists were unreasonable. Worse, anyone in the colonies who questioned British authority was considered a traitor. So in 1774 the British government passed the Navigation Acts. The goal was to gain more control of the colonies. Each act created a new tax.

The colonial battle cry became, "No taxation without representation!"

Tea was the first focus of colonial anger. For years, colonial merchants had been smuggling in low-quality tea. Then, in December 1773, British merchants sent tons of high-quality tea to Boston, Massachusetts. On purpose, the British priced the tea low enough to compete with the smuggled tea.

▲ the Boston Tea Party

Colonists did not want to buy the tea from the British—even though the quality was high. Many ports decided not to release the new tea for sale. Instead, the tea rotted on the docks.

One evening, Boston merchants decided to stage a protest. Many of the merchants had attended a town meeting led by colonist Samuel Adams. Adams urged the merchants to revolt. The English were especially afraid of the Mohawk Indian tribe. So the protesters dressed as Mohawks. Then, the "Indians" dumped every crate of tea into the sea. The protest became known as the Boston Tea Party. King George III heard about the protest and became furious. The king decided to punish anyone involved in the protest. The result was the Intolerable Acts.

Acts of Parliament 1763–1774

Name	Year	Intended Purpose	Result
Sugar Act	1764	to raise money to pay for soldiers in North America	The British government forced the colonists to pay duties on the molasses and sugar it received from such British colonies as the West Indies.
Currency Act	1764	Colonists wanted permission to print their own paper money.	The British government said no, that only British paper money could be used.
Stamp Act	1765	to raise money to pay for England's soldiers	This act required colonists to purchase special watermarked (or "stamped") paper for everything from legal documents to newspapers.
Quartering Act	1765	British troops living in the colonies needed places to live and food to eat.	The British government ruled that any unoccupied private home could be commandeered by troop leaders to use as a barracks. American colonists would pay a tax to help shelter and feed a certain number of soldiers.
Declaratory Act	1766	to punish protests and boycotts by colonists	The Stamp Act was repealed—a colonist victory—but this act declared that Britain had the right to issue any kind of tax it wanted.
Tea Act	1773	To raise money for England. The Tea Act lowered taxes on any tea shipped to the British colonies from the East India Tea Company, in order to undercut profits and compete with lower-priced smuggled tea.	the Boston Tea Party and other protests
Intolerable Acts	1774	Retribution for the colonists' continued rebellion against the British crown. These acts gave English courts the power to rule over legal matters in the colonies and select governing officials. The acts also closed down all Boston ports.	the Revolutionary War

Chapter 2

Fighting the French

Throughout history, England and France fought each other. Each country wanted to control the most powerful, or imperial (im-PEER-ee-ul), empire, or kingdom. In 1754 England and France fought the French and Indian War on American soil, where both countries ruled territories. Most Native Americans supported the French in battles with the British.

By the 1750s France had colonies in Canada. France also owned territory in Louisiana and along the Mississippi River. Just over 75,000 French colonists lived in America. The British claimed over 1.5 million colonists from Georgia up to Newfoundland in Canada.

The British and the French disagreed over everything. The French **brokered** (BROH-kerd), or negotiated to reach an agreement, an alliance with several Native American tribes. Together, the French and the Indians fought the vast British army and colonists. But France could not match the strength of England.

HISTORICAL PERSPECTIVE

The Sun Never Sets on the British Empire

"The sun never sets on the British Empire" was an expression made popular in the 1820s, but it was just as applicable in the 1700s. It meant that the English monarchy had dominion around the globe. The colonies—whether they were in the Americas, Africa, or Asia—were a critical part of Britain's economy and were also useful as strategic spots for military bases and trading ports.

▲ *The Death of General Wolfe* is a famous painting by Benjamin West depicting the death of James Wolfe, British commander of the French and Indian War.

Economic Causes of the Revolution

George Washington Fights for England

Fort Duquesne was a French military camp on the Ohio River. In 1753 a young colonial officer was involved in an event at the fort. The young man would one day lead the colonies to freedom in the Revolutionary War.

At the time, Robert Dinwiddie was the lieutenant governor of the Virginia Colony. Dinwiddie believed the French were trespassing on land that belonged to Virginia. So a twenty-two-year-old militia Virginia officer was sent to the fort to tell the French to leave the land that belonged to Virginia. The young officer on a first assignment was George Washington. The French would not meet with Washington, and a battle followed. The first battle of the French and Indian War had been fought.

PRIMARY SOURCE

The Journal of George Washington

George Washington kept detailed notes of his trip to ask the French to leave their post. Those notes became a journal, first published as a pamphlet in Williamsburg, Virginia. Later, it was reproduced in two installments of the *Maryland Gazette*. It is considered one of the most important documents in American history.

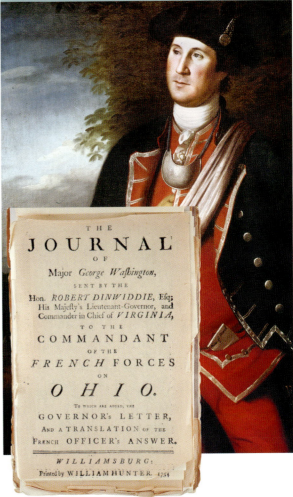

◀ This map shows the French territory in the seventeenth century, then called New France.

Chapter 2

The Spoils of War

The French and Indian War lasted from 1754 until 1763. The war went down in history as the first global conflict. Battles were fought in every British and French colony, on the seas and on land. Thousands of lives were lost.

The result of this conflict would have a major effect on America. Victory for England created the greatest colonial power in the world. But England was nearly bankrupt after defending claims to the colonies. And now England had a huge territory to protect. To get out of debt, England would have to tax the colonies heavily. England also would need to enforce the many trade laws that had been ignored for more than a century. Three thousand miles of ocean lay between England and the colonies, and England was distracted by other wars in Europe. For a long time, England had allowed the colonists to make many local decisions without consulting the British.

After the French and Indian War, the British wanted to keep the peace with Native Americans. So the king issued the Proclamation of 1763. The law restricted British settlement west of the Appalachian Mountains. Many colonists were angry because land to the west contained great promise. Colonists felt powerless, with no representation in Parliament. When England enforced

▲ The Proclamation of 1763, which banned further migration west of the Appalachians, increased tension between colonists and the crown.

old trade acts and passed new tax laws, colonists became enraged. The acts of rebellion that followed were the beginning of the Revolutionary War.

Economic Causes of the Revolution

Summing Up

- England benefited greatly from its colonies, charged high taxes on its goods, and limited the colonies' trade with other nations.

- The French and Indian War, and the pressure it put on England to raise money, was the leading economic cause of the American Revolution.

- The high tariffs and strict regulations without any colonial representative voice in British Parliament led to acts of rebellion and the popular slogan "No Taxation Without Representation."

Putting It All Together

Choose one of the following research activities. Work independently, in pairs, or in small groups. Share what you've learned with your class, and listen as others present their findings.

1 Use a blank map of the American colonies and fill in the names of each colony. Review what goods and services were provided by each colony. Make a key that represents goods and resources for each region.

2 Pretend you work for a newspaper during colonial times. Write an editorial where you explain your response to one of the acts of Parliament between 1763 and 1774.

3 Choose one of the Intolerable Acts. Which do you think was the hardest on the colonists? Why?

Checkpoint

Think About It

How are the results of the French and Indian War connected to the Acts of Parliament from 1763 to 1774?

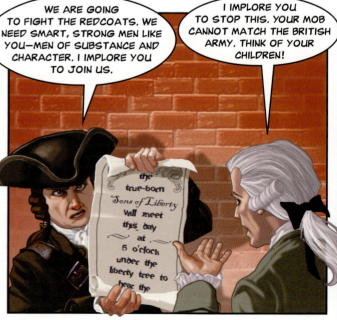

Chapter 3

Ideological Causes of the War

In the mid-1700s, a new, powerful series of ideas inspired people to believe in the right to independence. The ideas related to the word *intellectual*, which means "thinking logically and making use of ideas."

◀ Ben Franklin began his career as a printer.

What were the new ideas influencing people's thoughts about their right to independence?

ESSENTIAL VOCABULARY
- anonymously — page 40
- dictator — page 34
- Enlightenment — page 33
- philosopher — page 33

The Age of Enlightenment

To *enlighten* means "to inform or instruct, to find out something not previously known or considered."

In the movement called the Age of Enlightenment, **philosophers** (fih-LAH-suh-ferz), or thinkers, in Europe and the Americas expressed ideas in written articles, essays, and pamphlets. The philosophers talked about the importance of democracy, liberty, and freedom from oppression. The philosophers of the **Enlightenment** (in-LY-ten-ment) believed that science and reason made more sense than simply believing that the king and church were always right. In other words, science could be used to make the world a better place. Human beings could be in control of their own destiny.

In the past, a strict government was thought to be the will of God. Ideas in the Age of Enlightenment, such as the power of the individual, gave people a new understanding. People now believed in the right to oppose an oppressive government. People believed science could help to create a social plan to make the lives of people better.

The ideas seemed revolutionary at the time. But the concepts were not new. The principles of freedom and democracy were as old as ancient Greece and Rome.

HISTORY AND TECHNOLOGY

Although the printing press had been in use since the 1400s, advances in technology by the 1700s had made printing easier and cheaper. As a result, publications became available to anyone who cared to read them. Colonists were receiving their news from newspapers and pamphlets. This marked a huge change in society. Now everyone in a community, not just an elite group of wealthy individuals, could learn what was happening locally and all over the world. That is primarily how the ideas of the Enlightenment reached them.

Ancient Greece

In the ancient city of Athens, citizens founded the first democracy. Democracy means "rule by the people." In theory, all the people chose the leaders. In reality, only wealthy white men could vote in ancient Athens. However, all people had the right to voice their opinions.

Ancient Rome

In the Roman Republic, citizens did not want Rome to be led by a dictator (DIK-tay-ter), a person who rules with complete control. To avoid a dictator, leaders broke government into three parts. Each part, or branch, kept an eye on the other branches. The goal was to make sure one branch did not have too much power. Today the United States balances power with the same three branches of government.

Europe's Age of Enlightenment

John Locke (1632-1704)

John Locke was born in England to Puritan parents. After an education at Oxford University, Locke became a well-known doctor. John Locke saved the life of the Earl of Shaftesbury. Afterward, the earl helped Locke enter the world of politics and wealth. Locke strongly believed in liberty, free will, reason, tolerance, and the separation of church and state. He also thought there was a contract between government and the people that could not be broken. John Locke was a true supporter of the common person. Writings by Locke influenced great philosophers and the American revolutionaries.

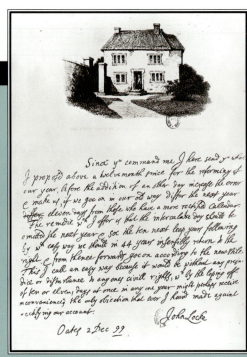

PRIMARY SOURCE

Locke's *Second Treatise of Government*

John Locke's massive written work *The Second Treatise of Government* had an enormous effect on the people who would soon declare their independence from Great Britain. In the section he called "On Tyranny," Locke spoke about the evils of oppression and the denial of rights. He was greatly influenced on these subjects by Isaac Newton, a scholar during the Age of Enlightenment known as the father of science. "A government is not free to do what it pleases . . . the law of nature, as revealed by Newton, stands as an eternal rule to all men . . . tyranny is the exercise of power beyond right, which no body can have a right to."

Ideological Causes of the War

John Locke

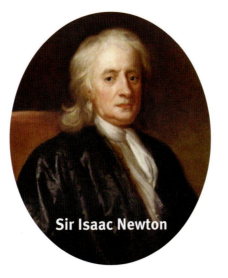
Sir Isaac Newton

Mary Wollstonecraft

Sir Isaac Newton (1642–1727)

Sir Isaac Newton was an English physicist and mathematician. Newton was a key figure in the scientific revolution. Newton invented calculus. The writings and discoveries by Newton laid the foundation for much of what is known about physics today. In the 1690s, he also began studying the Bible and questioning religion.

Mary Wollstonecraft (1759–1797)

Mary Wollstonecraft was a British writer and philosopher. Wollstonecraft also was an early supporter of rights for women. She is most famous for writing the pamphlet called *A Vindication of the Rights of Woman* (1792). The pamphlet argues that women are not inferior to men because of nature. Instead, Wollstonecraft wrote, a lack of education created inequality between women and men. Wollstonecraft felt that women should not be lesser members of the household. The writings of Mary Wollstonecraft caused much controversy. The writings also made a lasting impression on both women and men in the years to come

Newton, Wollstonecraft, and the other great thinkers in Europe proposed new ideals for people to think about.

Checkpoint
Think About It

What do terms like *rights*, *freedom*, and *liberty* mean to you?

Chapter 3

America's Brightest

The Age of Enlightenment started in Europe, but American colonists boasted many brilliant thinkers as well.

Thomas Jefferson (1743-1826)

Thomas Jefferson was a man of many talents. Today we know Jefferson as a writer, inventor, and politician. As a boy in Virginia, Jefferson was always curious and very, very smart. In college Jefferson studied law and languages. He was a devoted student of music and played both classical and folk music on the violin.

A college professor introduced Jefferson to the ideas of the Enlightenment. For Jefferson, those ideas went beyond the basics of liberty and freedom from tyranny. Jefferson believed in the strength of the common people. He believed that people who lived closest to nature understood best the meaning of being free.

After college Thomas Jefferson became involved in Virginia politics. Jefferson served in the Second Continental Congress. Soon, Jefferson, his friend Benjamin Franklin, and his sometime-rival John Adams were on a committee together. The men were asked to write a statement to declare the independence of America from England.

> **PRIMARY SOURCE**
>
> ### A Letter from Thomas Jefferson
>
> "Enlighten the people, generally, and tyranny of expressions and body and mind will vanish like spirits at the dawn of day."
>
> (1816 letter to his friend, French economist Pierre Samuel du Pont de Nemours)

Thomas Jefferson held many offices in government, including governor of Virginia, secretary of state for George Washington, and vice president to John Adams. Finally, in 1801, Thomas Jefferson was elected as the third president of the United States.

Although a group of men is credited with drafting the Declaration of Independence, it is believed that Thomas Jefferson was the main author of the document. ▶

Benjamin Franklin (1706-1790)

Benjamin Franklin was an American thinker, publisher, diplomat, scientist, and inventor. More than any other Founding Father, Franklin often traveled between the American colonies and Europe. In the United States, he played an important role in creating both the Declaration of Independence and the U.S. Constitution.

The Native American Influence

Colonists and Native Americans lived as neighbors—sometimes with respect and sometimes in fear of one another. Both groups of people shared ideas. For instance, the Native American system of governing strongly influenced European settlers.

The Iroquois (EER-oh-kwoi) Confederacy is one example. The Iroquois Confederacy was a union of tribes that stretched across the Atlantic coast. The Iroquois Constitution of the Five Nations set up a democratic government. The Iroquois government existed before the European explorers landed in North America. Later, colonists who wanted independence studied the Iroquois constitution. The document also inspired the writers of the United States Constitution.

◀ According to legend, Dekanawida (seated) helped establish the Iroquois Great Law, which later served as a guide for the framers of the United States Constitution.

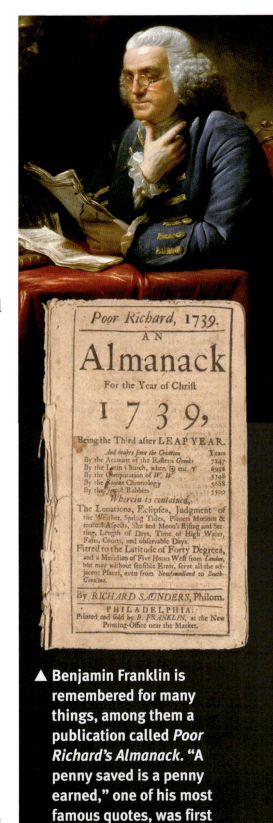

▲ Benjamin Franklin is remembered for many things, among them a publication called *Poor Richard's Almanack*. "A penny saved is a penny earned," one of his most famous quotes, was first printed in it.

Independence Is Declared!

The unfair treatment of the colonists by England and the new ideas of the Age of Enlightenment clashed. The settlers asked for reforms. England said no. The settlers asked for fair representation in British government. England turned the settlers down. The settlers asked for relief from taxes. There was none. The stage was set for the American Revolution.

On July 4, 1776, the Second Continental Congress read the Declaration of Independence to the colonies. The message was a warning shot to King George III.

HISTORICAL PERSPECTIVE

Freedom for All?

George Washington, Thomas Jefferson, and many other Founding Fathers supported freedom for all, but they also owned enslaved people. Although in his heart Jefferson knew that slavery was, as he put it, "an abominable crime," he did not mention independence for slaves in his Declaration. He knew if he said anything negative about slavery, the other southern delegates would never sign the Declaration of Independence.

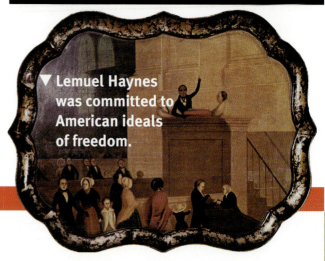

▼ Lemuel Haynes was committed to American ideals of freedom.

THEY MADE A DIFFERENCE

LEMUEL HAYNES (1753–1833)

When the men who wrote the Declaration of Independence dipped their quill pens into inkwells to sign the agreement that "all men are created equal," they weren't really talking about "all men." White, land-owning, business-running men were created equal. The same did not hold true for the enslaved Africans brought to American shores in chains.

Lemuel Haynes was an indentured servant in Massachusetts—not technically a slave but in many ways living like one. The key difference was that an indentured servant was required by law to be educated. Haynes was one of the few African American men of the period who could read and write.

Despite his own lack of real freedom, Haynes fought for the rights of others when he joined the Revolutionary Army. After the war, he wrote many pamphlets to spread his message: "Liberty is equally as precious to a black man, as it is to a white one, and bondage is equally as intolerable to the one as it is to the other."

Ideological Causes of the War

PRIMARY SOURCE

The Declaration of Independence, 1776
(EXCERPT)

When, in the course of human events, it becomes necessary for one people to dissolve the political bands which have connected them with another, and to assume among the powers of the earth, the separate and equal station to which the laws of nature and of nature's God entitle them, a decent respect to the opinions of mankind requires that they should declare the causes which impel them to the separation.

We hold these truths to be self-evident, that all men are created equal, that they are endowed by their Creator with certain unalienable rights, that among these are life, liberty and the pursuit of happiness . . .

Chapter 3

Thomas Paine's *Common Sense*

While the Declaration of Independence was making news, colonists were reading another document. The pamphlet was called *Common Sense*.

In England, Thomas Paine worked for the British government as a goods inspector. But Paine got fired. Paine worked as a schoolteacher and got fired. He opened a tobacco shop. The shop failed. Then, Thomas Paine moved to the American colonies. He worked as a journalist and newspaperman.

In January 1776, Thomas Paine published *Common Sense*. The pamphlet urged colonies to separate from England. Because Paine did not want to be jailed as a traitor, *Common Sense* was published **anonymously** (uh-NAH-nih-mus-lee), without showing the name of the author. The pamphlet sold well and helped sway the public opinion of colonists toward independence.

HISTORY AND LITERATURE

Common Sense

Thomas Paine's *Common Sense* fueled the fires of revolution by challenging England's right to power and demanding that oppression come to an end. Paine wrote: "As a long and violent abuse of power is generally the means of calling the right of it in question and as the king of England hath undertaken in his own right to support the parliament in what he calls theirs, and as the good people of this country are grievously oppressed by the combination, they have an undoubted privilege to inquire into the pretensions of both, and equally to reject the usurpations of either."

The Crisis

(published in December 1776; it also helped rally the Patriots)

These are the times that try men's souls. The summer soldier and the sunshine patriot will, in this crisis, shrink from the service of their country; but he that stands by it now, deserves the love and thanks of man and woman. Tyranny, like hell, is not easily conquered; yet we have this consolation with us, that the harder the conflict, the more glorious the triumph. What we obtain too cheap, we esteem too lightly: it is dearness only that gives every thing its value. Heaven knows how to put a proper price upon its goods; and it would be strange indeed if so celestial an article as FREEDOM should not be highly rated.

Ideological Causes of the War

Summing Up

- The Enlightenment was a period of great thinkers and written works that inspired the ideals of freedom and liberty.

- Men such as Thomas Jefferson and Thomas Paine used the ideals of the Enlightenment to urge the colonies to free themselves from British rule.

- The Declaration of Independence announced America's intention to fight its oppressors.

Putting It All Together

Choose one of the following research activities. Work independently, in pairs, or in small groups. Share what you've learned with your class, and listen as others present their findings.

1 Declare your independence. If you were going to start a new country, what rights would matter most to you and why?

2 Find out more about one of the figures of the Enlightenment. Are there other women and minorities whose contributions have been overlooked? How did they affect history?

3 Many government buildings in Washington, D.C. were inspired by Greek and Roman architecture. View pictures of buildings such as the U.S. Capitol or the Lincoln Memorial and compare them to pictures of the Parthenon in Greece or the Colosseum in Rome. Why did the builders in Washington choose those designs? Do you think they symbolize the belief that much of American history, our values and ideals, is an extension of Western civilization?

Checkpoint

Reread

Thomas Paine's *Common Sense* was written in the flowery parlance of the day. Break it down into modern language. What do you think it means?

Conclusion

A Triumphant Choice

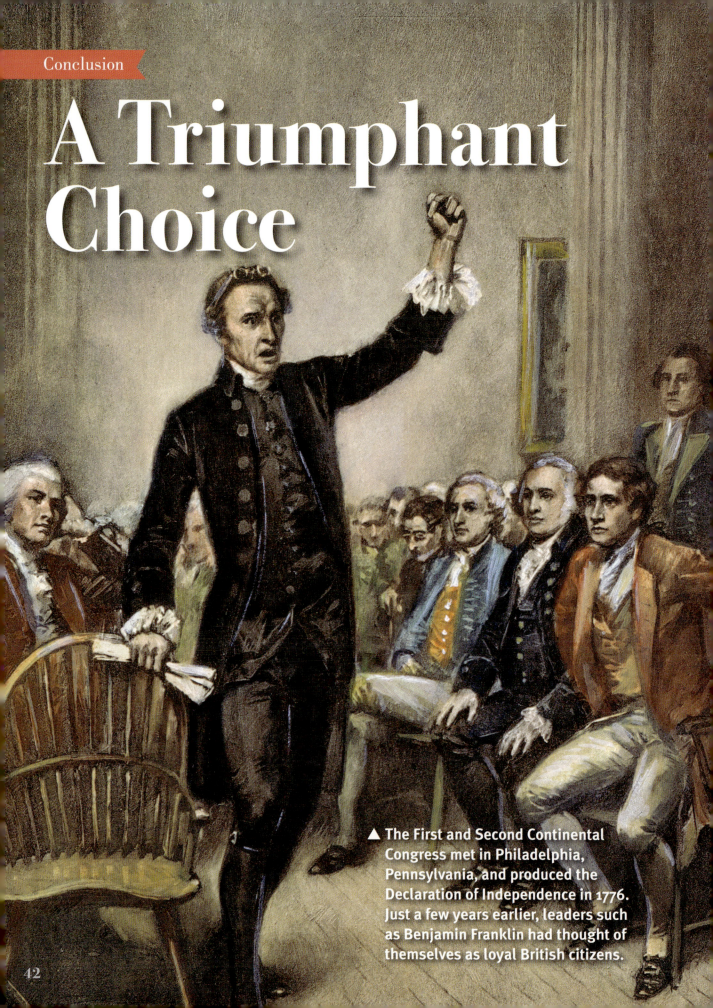

▲ The First and Second Continental Congress met in Philadelphia, Pennsylvania, and produced the Declaration of Independence in 1776. Just a few years earlier, leaders such as Benjamin Franklin had thought of themselves as loyal British citizens.

After the Boston Tea Party in 1773, King George said the colonists would have to submit to British taxation or triumph in a fight to end British rule. Within a few years, the colonies chose to fight. Soon the king faced a full rebellion. Colonists were not just fighting to end excessive taxation. The colonies rebelled against a government that would tax people who had no fair representation in the government. The colonists also were rising up against the British troops sent to the thirteen American colonies. To the colonists, the soldiers seemed to defend British economic interests, not the interests of the colonists.

By 1775, many colonists believed the ideas of the Enlightenment. The colonists were even used to some self-governing. The colonists wanted liberty and equality. They wanted a government that saw the worth of individuals. Colonists had helped fight and win the French and Indian War for Britain. So they believed that independence from Britain had been earned. Many colonists were now willing to die in order to bring an end to British tyranny.

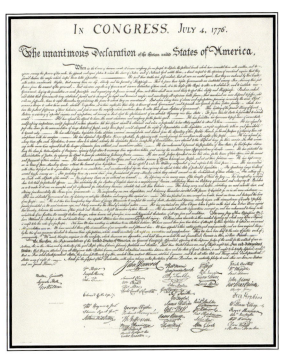

▲ **The Declaration of Independence explained why colonists had the right to be independent from England.**

▲ **The Royal British Navy had ships docked at the ports of all of its colonies. The ships' presence was a warning to the colonists: they were being watched and guarded at every moment.**

How to Write an Argument

1. Choose a topic that interests you. It should be a topic on which people have differing opinions.

2. Research the topic well. Find evidence and statistics on the topic.

3. Take a position on the topic based on your research.

4. Decide on the format and audience for your argument.

5. Outline your piece of writing.

6. Write a first draft.

    Remember a few tips:

    a. State your position and present a few strong reasons to support it.

    b. Write a clear paragraph to present each reason. Include evidence to support your position.

    c. Write a strong conclusion in which you restate your position.

7. Revise and proofread your writing. Are there presumptions in your argument that you need to support?

Loyalist Argument

The British colonies must remain loyal to the king. As we know all too well, a unified empire is a strong empire that benefits us all, promotes defense, and is good for trade, which is good for all. The cost of being part of a great empire is that we must follow British law and pay British taxes. Without this contract between the people and the government, our society is not sustainable and we will have nothing but chaos.

The crown came to our aid and protected us from the French and Indian groups who would have taken our lands and our livelihoods. It is our solemn duty to repay that debt and not ask for representation on the other side of the world, which would be, above all else, impractical.

Patriot Argument

People are born with certain rights—a right to live, to be free, to own land, to prosper, and even to pursue their interests. We believe in forming a government that cannot tread on these rights and that cannot take our hard-earned property by way of unlawful and unfair taxation. We must rise up against a government that would levy a tax on its people without fair representation in that government body. And since a great ocean exists between us and that government, and we do not feel that we would ever be sufficiently represented in such a Parliament, we must establish our own government, on our own land—a government of the people, by the people, and for the people. We fought alongside the redcoats for this land in the French and Indian War, and now those British troops by order of their king are turning on us. We must fight back. They have given us no other acceptable choice.

Glossary

anonymously — (uh-NAH-nih-mus-lee) *adverb* unidentified by choice (page 40)

banishment — (BA-nish-ment) *noun* the state of being exiled or cast out of one's home country (page 10)

broker — (BROH-ker) *verb* to negotiate (page 26)

dictator — (DIK-tay-ter) *noun* a ruler with absolute power (page 34)

Enlightenment — (in-LY-ten-ment) *noun* a movement in the eighteenth century centered on the critical and scientific examination of old beliefs (page 33)

frontier — (frun-TEER) *noun* border between settled and unsettled areas (page 12)

imperial — (im-PEER-ee-ul) *adjective* relating to an empire or kingdom (page 26)

indentured servant — (in-DEN-cherd SER-vunt) *noun* someone bound to work by legal contract for a specified number of years in payment of a debt (page 11)

indigo — (IN-dih-goh) *noun* blue dye obtained from several species of the *Indigofera* plant (page 21)

Loyalist — (LOY-uh-list) *noun* a person who remained loyal to Great Britain during the American Revolution (page 14)

mercantilism — (MER-kun-ty-lih-zum) *noun* economic system in which governments strictly regulate the buying and selling of goods and create colonies to further the country's monetary wealth (page 19)

monarchy — (MAH-nar-kee) *noun* a form of government in which a sole, absolute, and royal individual rules the state or country (page 8)

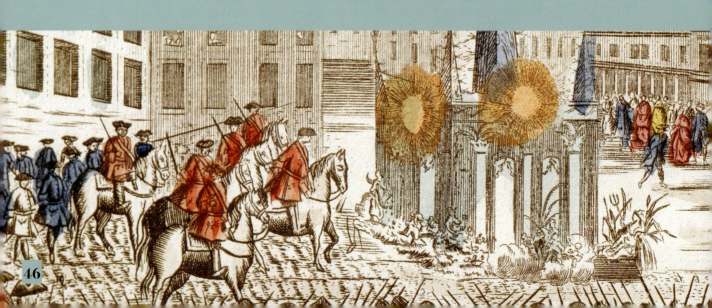

oppression	(uh-PREH-shun) *noun* cruel or unjust treatment at the hands of an authority (page 24)	
Patriot	(PAY-tree-ut) *noun* one who sided with the thirteen colonies during the Revolutionary War (page 14)	
persecution	(per-sih-KYOO-shun) *noun* the hostile or ill treatment of a group or individual (page 8)	
philosopher	(fih-LAH-suh-fer) *noun* a thinker or scholar (page 33)	
Pilgrim	(PIL-grim) *noun* a religious Separatist from England who settled in Plymouth (page 8)	
plantation	(plan-TAY-shun) *noun* a large farming estate usually worked by resident labor (page 22)	
prosperity	(prah-SPAIR-ih-tee) *noun* a condition of thriving economically (page 11)	
revolution	(reh-vuh-LOO-shun) *noun* a forced overthrow of a government in order to create a better one (page 16)	
tariff	(TAIR-if) *noun* a system of taxes on imported or exported goods (page 19)	
theocracy	(thee-AH-kruh-see) *noun* a government in which rulers are regarded as divinely guided (page 10)	
theologian	(thee-uh-LOH-jun) *noun* a person who studies religious beliefs and practices (page 10)	
tolerance	(TAH-luh-runs) *noun* peaceful coexistence of people with differing beliefs or practices (page 10)	

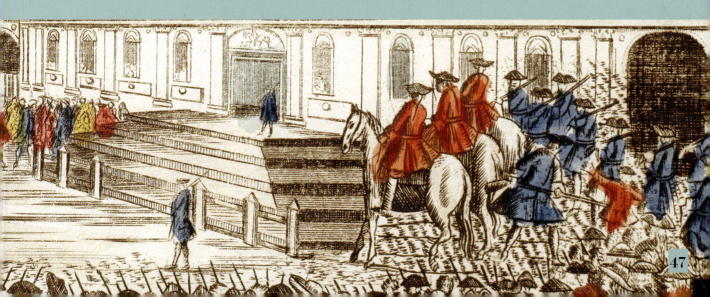

Index

Acts of Parliament, 25
Adams, John, 30, 36
Age of Enlightenment, 33–34, 36–38
anonymous, 40
banishment, 10
broker, 26
Canada, 23, 26
Cayuga, 23
Church of England, 8
Common Sense, 40
Continental Congress, First, 5, 16, 42
Continental Congress, Second, 36, 38, 42
Currency Act, 25
Declaration of Independence, 16, 36–41
Declaratory Act, 25
dictator, 34
Dutch East India Company, 11
Enlightenment, 33–38, 41, 43
Fort Duquesne, 27
France, 23, 26–27
Franklin, Benjamin, 36–37
French and Indian War, 12, 14, 26, 43
frontier, 12
Greece, ancient, 33–34

Haynes, Lemuel, 38
Hudson, Henry, 11
Hutchinson, Anne, 10
imperial, 26
indentured servant, 11, 38
indigo, 21
Intolerable Acts, 16, 24–25
Iroquois Nation (Confederacy), 23, 37
Jefferson, Thomas, 36, 38, 41
King George III, 5, 14, 16, 24, 38, 43
Locke, John, 34
Locke's *Second Treatise on Government*, 34
Loyalist, 14, 31, 45
Mayflower, 8
mercantilism, 19, 21
Middle Passage, 20
Mohawk, 23–24
monarchy, 8, 26
Native Americans, 10, 12, 17, 23, 26, 28, 37
New Netherland, 11
Newton, Sir Isaac, 34–35
Oneida, 23
Onondaga, 23
oppression, 24, 33–34, 40
Paine, Thomas, 40–41

Patriot, 14, 40, 45
Penn, William, 10
persecution, 8, 10
philosopher, 33
Pilgrims, 8, 10
plantation, 22
prosperity, 11, 17
Puritans, 9–10, 34
Quartering Act, 14, 25
revolution, 16, 36
Rome, ancient, 33–34
Seneca, 23
Stamp Act, 14–15, 25
Sugar Act, 14, 25
tariff, 5, 19, 24, 29
Tea Act, 25
theocracy, 10
theologian, 10
tolerance, 10, 17, 34
Triangle Trade, 20–21
tyranny, 24, 34, 36, 43
U.S. Constitution, 37
Warren, Mercy Otis, 15
Washington, George, 13, 23, 27, 36, 38
Williams, Roger, 10
Wollstonecraft, Mary, 35

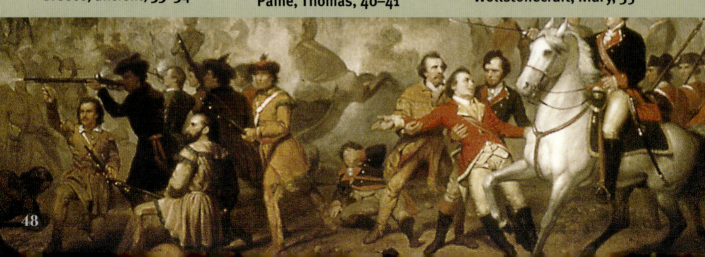